Choose a topic and start to practise writing. Each booklet has a theme to help you start to write…stories, reports, articles, letters and many more. Start collecting them now.

Guinea Pig Creative Writing booklets also provide extra practice for children who have completed:

- Creative Story Writing ISBN: 9780955831508
- Persuasive Writing & Argument ISBN: 9780955831515
- Information Writing ISBN: 9780955831522

They are for:

* children who are working at Key Stage 2 of the National Curriculum, levels 3-5 (in Years 5 and 6 of primary school),
* children who are working at Key Stage 3, levels 3-5 (Years 7 and 8 of Secondary School).

They provide practice for all 9-13 year olds, especially children taking 11+ examinations.

Let's **learn** to *write* <u>fiction</u>.

When you *write fiction*, <u>**you must**</u>:

1. Decide who will be your audience?

2. Think of different genres – realistic, detective, ghost, gothic horror.

3. Ask what is the purpose of my writing?

When you *write to entertain*, remember that <u>**you must**</u> :

1. Have an interesting opening and a memorable ending

2. Have good characters, setting and plot

3. Build up suspense

4. Use dialogue – to move the story along

5. Use a variety of simple, compound and complex sentences

Plan your fiction writing:

PARAGRAPH 1 • Start with a memorable first sentence to make the reader want to read on. • Introduce the characters and the setting. • Introduce the plot.	**Write:** • in **FIRST PERSON**, so you are the main character telling the story (using I or we) or • in **THIRD PERSON** (using he or she) as if you were a fly watching from the wall.
PARAGRAPH 2 • Develop the plot. • What might happen to trigger off a series of events? • Build up suspense. **PARAGRAPH 3** • Wind up your story with a good ending. In the resolution you will have solved all the problems. • It could be happy, sad, a cliff hanger (which leaves the reader to make up his or her own mind), or a moral ending • Have a memorable final sentence.	**Remember:** • Use connectives or conjunctions: - *and or but (to join compound sentences)* - *or, so, if, when, while, after, before, because, unless, until, whereas, although (to join complex sentences)* - *use pronouns - who, which, whose, what, that* - *to link ideas use - firstly, later, therefore, on the other hand, at that moment, by this time, next, soon...* • Use a range of sentences – simple, compound and complex sentences

Here is a plan for a story.

<table>
<tr>
<td>

<u>Characters</u>:

- *Frank accompanied by Dad.*

</td>
<td>

<u>Setting</u>:

- *They are walking down the High Street on a shopping trip.*

</td>
</tr>
</table>

1. Frank sees a shop closing down. An exciting new computer game is greatly reduced in the shop window. It is half price.

2. Introduce the Plot: Frank grabs Dad's arm, "Look, that new game is in the sale. It is the one they advertise on T.V. Can we get one?"

3. They reluctantly join the queue and wait for half an hour for the shop to open and for the sale to start.

4. A shop assistant starts to unlock the door. Everyone starts to talk excitedly. The door is open wide. Everyone rushes towards the door.

5. They run in towards the electronic department. A huge crowd is racing towards the pile of games. The manager is shouting.

6. Everyone is grabbing and pushing each other out of the way. Hundreds of hands are reaching out, clutching at the boxes. Frank reaches for the last box. Another person grabs it too. "You can't have this one, it's mine," shouts Frank angrily.

"No, it's mine," says the girl stubbornly

What is the *outcome*?

- Frank leaves the shop in tears with no game, but Dad promises to buy the game from another store.

- The other person politely gives in, saying Frank can buy the game.

- The shop keeper produces another game from the window.

- A huge fight breaks out. A policeman is called.

Characters:

- *Dad:* ....
  ....
- *Frank: dressed in his casual clothes and shiny new trainers.*
- ● ....
  ....

Setting:

- *Where are they?*
- *Describe the scene in the High Street:* ....
  ....
  ....
  ....

---

1. **What does Frank see?**
   (Opening of story)

   ....
   ....
   ....
   ....
   ....
   ....
   ....

2. **What does he do?**

   ....
   ....
   ....
   ....
   ....
   ....
   ....

3. **What does he say to dad?**

   ....
   ....
   ....
   ....
   ....
   ....
   ....

4. **What happens next?**
   (Develop the story)

   ....
   ....
   ....
   ....
   ....
   ....
   ....

5. Describe how he ran into the toy shop to get a half price computer game. By the time he gets to the department, there is only one box left. As he reaches out to get it, a girl grabs it off him. Who grabbed it? Why?

(Is there a complication?)

....

....

....

....

....

....

....

6. ... And after that? What adds to the excitement and builds up suspense? (Crisis)

....

....

....

....

....

....

....

7. ...And then?

....

....

....

....

....

....

8. What is the outcome? How are events resolved? Did he get the game or did he go home without one? What did Dad say? How did he feel? Did he get one: from the internet, as a present for his birthday or did he decide not to get one?

(Resolution) ....

....

....

....

Closing Down Sale

Every Saturday morning, Dad took Frank into town after swimming while Mum worked. They would potter around the market, buy fruit and vegetables, get a milk shake from the fast food place and look in the shop windows as they strolled back up to the multi storey car park. That particular morning, something grabbed Frank's attention. It was a huge sign draped outside a store, which read 'Closing Down Sale', in big black bold letters. This shop sold computer games like the one he wanted. Frank was curious so he tugged Dad's arm, "Can we have a look?" he begged, looking at him pleadingly.

"OK, replied Dad," glancing at his watch. "If we're quick."

A huge crowd had formed outside the store, waiting for the shop to open. Frank peered closely into the window. They had the latest computer game in there…and it was reduced to a crazy low price. "I have to get one," pleaded Frank, nudging Dad. "If you put it on your debit card, I'll pay you back with money from my savings account… I promise."

"Well, that's certainly an amazing bargain," replied Dad. They waited in a huge queue of people for ten minutes, until a flustered shop assistant opened the door. The crowd surged forward. People were shoving and pushing to get to the front. Frank squeezed through – and as the door opened – he ran with the fastest people. The race was on and he zoomed up the escalator to the third floor: running, puffing and panting. There, he caught sight of a pile of boxes containing the latest computer games, but they were going rapidly. Five, four, three, two… He grabbed firmly hold of the last box, but someone else snatched it from him. It was a tall girl, with blue jeans and a yellow fleece. Frank saw red as he felt anger rise in him and he seized it back. The girl with eyes like black pools, stared at him with malice.

"It's mine," Frank protested in a raised voice.

"No it's not. That's not fair," she retaliated. "I was here first."

"That's completely out of order," Frank insisted, going red in the face.

"It's mine," the girl repeated, bursting into floods of tears.

At that point a red-faced manager, in a dark suit, strolled over. He saw the hysterical girl and acting on impulse, made a swift decision. He took the computer game from Frank and said to the girl that he would wrap it for her at the till. "But, I had it first, really I did," Frank protested indignantly.

"I don't think so," snarled the irate shop manager and walked away purposefully. Frank was gob smacked; his dream was smashed. As Dad arrived panting, Franks own eyes were welling up with fat tears that dripped heavily down his face and fell on the floor like raindrops. It hurt! It was unjust!

"That's unfair," he tried to explain to Dad.

"Things are not always fair in this world explained Dad. Sometimes you just have to let things go."

A little while later, Frank and Dad pulled up on the drive of their house. Frank got out of the car slowly, weighed down by a sad, depressed feeling. Mabel was outside. She was Frank's elderly next-door neighbour and she was carrying some bulging bags home from the supermarket. She smiled and waved in her usual cheery way. "What's up dear?" she beamed. "You look glum, as though you're carrying all the world's problems on your young shoulders. Dear me! Anyway, I'm glad I've caught you. I wanted to see you, dear. I've got something that will cheer you up." She beckoned him into her tidy hall. "You've been so kind to me recently, helping me in my garden. I've really appreciated what you and your Dad have done for me: cutting my lawn and weeding my flower borders. I'm so grateful; I want to give you something in return. You see, dear, I won this in a competition, but I've got no use for it myself and no family to give it to so I want you to have it."

"No we don't need anything Mabel, really, we don't!" insisted Frank.

"No, I insist dear." She handed him a smart carrier bag. He peered inside. It was a computer game, the one he wanted. He almost leapt in the air and then he did something that he had never done before. He gave Mabel a big hug to say thank you. He turned to go, clutching the bag. Events had taken an unexpected twist. Did she know what had happened at the shop, he thought? How could she have known? At that moment, it seemed more important to help his elderly neighbour than play games on his computer. "Thanks again Mabel," he shouted over his shoulder. "I'll be round next Saturday to plant your bulbs for next spring."

Write your own story called 'The Closing Down Sale'.

<u>Can I have that game?</u>

When a story is written as a play script, the dialogue of the characters comes alive because you can see them acting out the story on the stage. In this scene, Frank is persuading his Dad that he should be allowed to go into the game store that is closing down. Your task is to continue the play script.

<u>**Scene 1:**</u>	*(In the High Street or in the shopping mall.)*
Frank:	What's that big notice up there, Dad, the one in big bold letters?
Dad:	I think it says, 'Closing Down Sale' but I'm not wearing my glasses. It looks like it is the last day.
Frank:	Can we have a look round the store?
Dad:	I think we've got time *(looking at his watch)*
	They cross the road and walk over to the shop, joining a big crowd. Frank pushes his way to the front and peers into the window.
Frank:	Look at all those computer games? It says, 'reduced to clear'.
Dad:	That's a good price.
Frank:	Please Dad. *(Frank looks expectantly at his father.)* Please, please can I have one?
	(Dad looks perplexed.)
Dad:	Well, I'll put it on my debit card, if you promise to pay me back. It's a lot of money even half price.
Frank	I'll get some money out of my savings account to pay for it. I promise.
Dad:	Ok, we'll have a look.
First lady in crowd:	*(fidgeting about impatiently.)* It must be nearly time to open. It's gone 9 o' clock
Second lady in crowd:	I can see the assistant just coming over now to unlock the door.
First lady in crowd:	Come on then, love. Let's get to the front so we can get the best bargains.
Frank:	Come on Dad, let's push our way to the front.

| **Dad:** | You run ahead. You can run faster than me. Choose what you want and I'll be up there in a few minutes. |

(The assistant unlocks the door and it swings open. The crowd surge forward and people begin to rush in. Frank runs with the fastest people.)

| **Member of crowd:** | Mind out of the way |

| **Another member of crowd:** | Do you mind? |

| ***Member of crowd:*** | I'm sure you poked me with your umbrella. |

| ***Another member of crowd:*** | I'm sorry, I didn't mean to. |

| **Girl in yellow fleece:** | There's the game department over there. It's got some incredible bargains. |

(The people run as fast as their legs will carry them. They start to grab the boxes, but the big pile goes down quickly. When Frank arrives, there are only two left.)

<u>Scene 2</u>

> Write your version of the play script from here. What happens between the girl in the yellow fleece and Frank? Read on to see how the play could continue.

....

....

....

....

....

....

....

....

....

....

....

....

....

....

....

....

<u>**Scene 2**</u>

(On the third floor of the shop that's closing down, Frank has grabbed the last box but a girl in a yellow fleece tries to snatch it off him.)

Frank

I only just made it. I'll take the last one.

Girl in yellow fleece:

That's mine!

Frank:

I got it first.

Girl in yellow fleece:

No you didn't. *(She snatches it off him.)* I was here before you. It's mine, mine, mine. *(She screeches out the words, getting louder and becoming increasingly red in the face.)* *(Frank, seeing red, grabs it back.)*

Frank:

It certainly is not yours. I've been here ages. I was just waiting for my Dad to…

Girl in yellow fleece:

It's mine.
Boo, Boo, Boo! *(Girl starts to sob loudly.)*

(The assistant approaches the scene.)

Assistant:

What's going on here? Is this young man causing you some trouble?

Frank:

I had it first. That's out of order.

Assistant:

I've been observing from the till and I'm not so sure about that. You need to learn some manners. *(The assistant has an angry tone of voice and directs his comments towards Frank.)* Give it to me. It's obvious this girl had it first and you have snatched it from her. *(The assistant turns to the girl and gives her the box.)*

Assistant:

Take it to the till, my dear, and pay for it quickly. *(Turning towards Frank he says…)* Run along boy and don't cause me any more trouble.

(Dad, a bit breathless, arrives on the scene.)

Dad:

What's up?

Frank:

(exploding with rage and bright red in the face)
I took that box, but the girl came and grabbed it off me. I snatched it back, but the shop assistant has sided with her - and has given it back to her - and is wrapping it up for her right now. It's not fair. It's unjust. He can't do that.

(Frank's indignation is shown by his eyes welling up and tears dripping down his face.)

Frank:

It's not fair.

Dad:

Things are not always fair. Sometimes you just have to let things go. Come on, let's go back to the car or we'll get a ticket.

(Frank strolls quietly beside Dad, his cheeks still flushed, his pride still hurt.)

A play is performed on the stage in front of an audience.

What does a play script have?

It has:

- **DIALOGUE** between characters to show:

    - how they relate to each other
    - how they feel
    - how characters react to the things that happen

At an exciting point in the play, dramatic tension is built up, to make the audience sit up on the edge of their seats.

- **PUNCTUATION**: use a colon after the characters name.

Frank: *It's not fair.*

Dad: *Things are not always fair. Sometimes you have to let things go.*

- **STAGE DIRECTIONS** in <u>italics</u> and brackets.

(Dad entered breathless)

The stage directions indicate:

    - where the play is set (in the High Street)
    - where the scene takes place.

    - the actions of characters – to show what they do, other things that happen and what happens around them.

(looking at his watch)   *(the crowd surge forward)*

    - how characters feel

(Dad looked perplexed)

Use the story to write scene 3 of the play script.

<u>Scene 3</u>

(Enter drive and park car.)

Frank: I still think that was really mean – what the assistant did to me.

Dad: You must try to forget it.

Frank: No! I can't. He took that game away from me and gave it to that girl. He knew I had the money in my hand. It was an injustice. You could write one of your letters.

Dad: I could but it won't do any good. We'll just get some nice reply saying how sorry they are. What's the point? It won't undo what's happened. Try and think of something else. Look there's Mabel, wave to her.

Frank: She's coming over.

Dad: How's it going Mabel? How's your bad knee? Those bags look heavy. Let me carry those for you.

Mabel: No, don't worry dear. They're not too bad.

Dad: Come on. I insist.

Mabel: Thank you. You're so good, but anyway I wanted to see this young man.

Dad: They weigh a tonne! I don't know how you got them home.

Mabel: Frank, what's up dear? You look so glum! You look like you've carrying all the world's problems on your shoulders.

Frank: Nothing, really.

Dad: Had a tiring week at school.

Mabel: Well I wanted a word. I've got something that might just cheer you up.

Frank   *(Looking puzzled.)*   What's that Mabel?

Mabel: Anyway, I'm so glad I caught you dear. You've been so kind to me recently - helping me in my garden. I've really appreciated what you and your Dad have done for me, cutting my lawn and weeding the flowerbeds. I'm so grateful. I want to give you something in return.

Frank: We don't need anything Mabel!

Mabel: No, I insist. Come into my hall, just for a minute.
It's in that bag by the table. Can you get it for me dear?

(Frank carries a smart carrier bag over to Mabel.)

Frank: It looks exciting!

Mabel: It is, dear. Let's undo the string. If I lift it up a bit, you'll be able to see what it is. You'll know more about these than me.

Frank: *(Peering in)*
A computer game...

<table>
<tr><td>Mabel:</td><td>Yes dear. I won it in that competition at Fresco. It was just a draw but I thought I'd buy a ticket. Then I had a letter come to say I'd won. Me... Won! I said to myself I've never won anything before!</td></tr>
<tr><td>Frank:</td><td>It's so cool. It's like this...</td></tr>
<tr><td>Dad:</td><td>It's the same model as...</td></tr>
<tr><td>Mabel:</td><td>I'd like you to have it dear. I'm much to old to be bothered to learn how to use it. My eye sights not what it used to be. I've got no one to give it to. You know, I've got no family now. Please take it, dear.</td></tr>
<tr><td>Frank:</td><td>(She hands him the bag)
Wow, I don't know what to say.</td></tr>
<tr><td>Dad:</td><td>Are you sure? You could sell it.</td></tr>
<tr><td>Mabel:</td><td>No. I can't be bothered with that at my age. You have it and enjoy it.</td></tr>
<tr><td>Dad:</td><td>If you're sure.</td></tr>
<tr><td>Mabel:</td><td>Yes I am.</td></tr>
<tr><td>Frank:</td><td>Thank you so much. It's great. It's amazing. It's incredible. I can't find the words. It's just what I wanted. (Frank is leaping up and down.) Thank you Mabel. Thank you so much. (He hugs Mabel.)</td></tr>
<tr><td>Dad:</td><td>You really don't know how you've made his day. I won't go into the story now, but he'd set his heart on one...</td></tr>
<tr><td>Cat:</td><td>meow, meow, meow</td></tr>
<tr><td>Mabel:</td><td>Enjoy! Enjoy! Better get this lot away and feed the cat.</td></tr>
<tr><td>Frank:</td><td>Thank you, Mabel. Next week you can pop in and help me play on it.</td></tr>
<tr><td>Mabel:</td><td>You cheeky monkey!</td></tr>
<tr><td>Frank:</td><td>(aside to himself)
Did she know what had happened at the shop? No, how could she.
(calling over his shoulder)
Thanks again, Mabel. I'll be round to plant your spring bulbs next Saturday.</td></tr>
</table>

How do people feel?

Make some notes on the reasons why the girl in the yellow fleece might want the computer game? Why did she behave like she did?

....

....

....

....

....

How did Frank feel when the assistant gave the girl his game?

....

....

....

....

How did Mabel feel about Frank and his Dad?

....

....

....

....

What did Sam feel like when he opened Mabel's present?

....

....

....

....

How does Dad feel? What could he tell Frank's mum?

....

....

....

....

Look up the following words in the dictionary.

Describe the shop?

> *crazy* low *prices*, <u>reductions</u>, **amazing bargains**, a poster draped across the entrance.

Can you think of some crowd words?

> *crowds*, <u>pushing & shoving</u>, grabbing & squeezing, clutching, **grabbing up bargains**, snatching, <u>seizing</u>, grasping, *reductions*

How does Frank feel?

> sad, **bursts into tears**, *wells up*, tears dripping, *goes red*, <u>feels indignation,</u> **says it is unfair**, feels hard done by.

People:

> accompany each other, *potter about*, insist, beckon, plead, <u>screech</u>, protest, are reluctant, **act on impulse**, be grateful, appreciate.

Find some more words by looking in a thesaurus. Write them on this page.

Persuade people to *buy* a game...

An innovative games' company has brought out a super new, virtual electronics game. To tell people about the game, the manufacturer wants to produce an advertisement for T.V.

Your task is to write the advertisement to convince people to buy one.

Before you start. Think about the answers to these questions:

- Who is it aimed at? What age range?

  (We call this the target audience.)

- What is the purpose?
- What is the name of the game?
- What is the aim of the game?
- How do you play the game?
- Why is this game so exciting?
- Why is this game better than other games in the shops?

INVENT A SUPER SONIC JET THAT FLIES FIFTY TIMES THE SPEED OF SOUND. PILOT THIS INNOVATION. DETERMINE HOW FAR YOU CAN TRAVEL INTO THE INTERGALACTIC WORLD. GO BEYOND... GO TO WHERE NO ONE HAS EVER BEEN BEFORE... GO INTO DEEP SPACE... INTO OTHER GALAXIES... AND OTHER UNIVERSES. FIND OUT WHAT LAYS BEYOND THE STARS AND PLANETS.

RELEASED ON: September 15th 2020

Reserve you copy now, at all good stores.

Use these ideas to help you write your advert.

Imagine:

What would you be able to do in this game?

....

....

....

....

What would the journey to outer space be like?

....

....

....

What obstacles would you have to overcome on the way there?

....

....

....

....

Who would you meet? What kind of aliens? Would they be dangerous?

....

....

....

....

How would the game work? What would be your ultimate goal to reach?
If you reached it, what would you see?

....

....

....

Who would the game be for? What is the purpose of it?

....

....

....

Hi Fli Spy Games present...

LION LOVE

Rear your own lion cub. Wean him with bottled milk. Watch him grow. Teach him to hunt. Hold him tight.

Released on: ....
Reserve a copy.

Hi Fli Spy Games present...

SET UP A SAFARI PARK or ZOO

Plan out the park. Choose the animals. Employ staff. Experience running your own park. Feed and care for your animals.

Hi Fli Spy Games present...

'LET'S SPY ON CAREERS' SERIES

BE A FIREMAN

Great for helping you decide which career to choose. The ultimate work experience opportunity. Your chance to establish your own virtual career as a fire fighter. See what it is like to be called out to fight a fire. See how you would cope when the heat is intense, when danger approaches and when fear overwhelms you.

Which careers would be included in this series?

- Policeman
- Lawyer
- Plumber
- Lorry Driver...

Can you think of any more?

Hi Fli Spy Games present...

SET UP YOUR OWN HOTEL

Find a sight. Plan and design the rooms. Welcome your guests. Deal with the day to day running of your hotel.

Hi Fli Spy Games present...

DRIVE IN A DRIVING COMPETITION

You will be judged on your driving and award points for your technique.

Released on: ....
Reserve a copy.

Hi Fli Spy Games present...

DESIGN YOUR OWN FASHION LABEL.

Become a fashion designer. Create your collection of stunning creations. Create a fashion show and watch your models present your designs to the world.

Released on: ....
Reserve a copy.

Made in the USA
Monee, IL
07 July 2026

56552030R00015